Ground Effect
After Spin Recovery

poems by

Betsy Lynch

Finishing Line Press
Georgetown, Kentucky

Ground Effect
After Spin Recovery

Copyright © 2025 by Betsy Lynch
ISBN 979-8-89990-205-5 First Edition

All rights reserved under International and Pan-American Copyright Conventions. No part of this book may be reproduced in any manner whatsoever without written permission from the publisher, except in the case of brief quotations embodied in critical articles and reviews.

Publisher: Leah Huete de Maines
Editor: Christen Kincaid
Cover Art: Ausable Chasm, taken by Madison Walling
Interior Art: Betsy Lynch
Author Photo: Ed Sterba
Cover Design: Elizabeth Maines McCleavy

Order online: www.finishinglinepress.com
also available on amazon.com

Author inquiries and mail orders:
Finishing Line Press
PO Box 1626
Georgetown, Kentucky 40324
USA

Contents

Photo: Our little Tomahawk "Shadow fax" (Gandolph's horse) 1

Still Seeking Home 2

Here 3

Spin Recovery: Hard Opposite Rudder, Yoke Down 4

The Arrival of Childhood's End: Sci-fi Becomes Fact, Place 9

Septembers Flipbook Scenes, Flash Before the End 10

Photo: Point au Roche, Lake Champlain 12

Steadfast Cedars at Point au Roche Middle Point 13

Trashcan Turkey 14

Alas It Was to None but Me 15

Photo: Passage Key, off Anna Maria Island 16

Sunny Angel Wings 17

Photo: Lake Champlain, Valcour Island 18

Reflections on Brochure of Home: Lake Champlain's
 Adirondack Coast 19

And the Greatest of These is Love 22

Pantomime of the Doomed Mango Tree 23

Photo: Rattlesnake Mountain/ Lake Champlain 25

Clarity 26

Taking My Morning Vitamins 27

Ground Effect2: Conversation with the One Who Knew Me Best,
 Once He's Gone, Please Forgive Me the Shock 28

Photo: Aerial Flight Tampa Bay 29

How to Survive a Hurricane from Far, Far Away 30

Reference Points: After the Hurricane 31

Photo: Whiteface Overlook 32

We Uprooted Souls Seek 33

This collection is dedicated to my deceased brother, William Farel Mullen, and his three boys, Cris, Andrew, Nicholas. Patty, Ken, and Ryan have nurtured them along with many others. His niece and nephew, Heidi and Finn, remember his eccentricity and humor. Farel was a writer, restauranteur, hotel manager, among other jobs, living in "Hemingway Country", Florida Keys prior to his premature end.

My dearest aunt said, during her last nursing home days,

"I want to go home. But I don't know where that is."

Our Little Tomahawk, "Shadow fax" (Gandolph's horse)

Still Seeking Home

When I was a child, my brother a few years older,

made a pretend airplane with wings

(carboard affixed to canoe, dashboard made of TV dinner trays)

In our backyard in Sparta, New Jersey, on Springbrook Trail.

We wanted to fly

sitting in that fabrication.

The family disease drove us outside,

drove him to shortchange many aspirations,

drove me into spins both real and metaphorical.

Over decades, we rescued, lied, covered up

for each other and our parents, left havoc.

Amidst the wreckage, a few of us recovered.

Today I fly for real.

Still seeking home.

Here

In this moment
past the rush
of flight through clouds,
past the faint scent of electrical heat,
past lush measured
fields of myriad greens,
over oval hard dirt horse tracks,
fancy red barns, clean white silos,
long white fences, fruit orchards
reaching up, out to sun's power,
my power-off descent gentle,
soft landing on grass runway,
after I push

the little plane into its hangar,

final silence

here

is the ache

I sought to escape,

the wait near the phone

for busy adult children

here and here

the world's violence crushes me.

I want to speak,

to listen to them,

to love.

Spin Recovery: Hard Opposite Rudder, Yoke Down

1

I'd listened to an eloquent retired F-16 pilot recount joy
at atmosphere's edge, a shelf above the Saudi mountain range,

a thin line dividing vast black velvet, star-sprinkled,

against white shadow-dazzled desert.
Oh my God, I want to do that!

2

A post career obsession had me
piloting solo, a friend's small plane
over a Gulf paradise island,
its swirling white sandbars
current-carved as though by
a contemplative god,
casually mixing aqua seas, stirring white sand
with a thousand blues and greens.
Shadows of dolphin schools
gently arced
near the tiny marine pilot base
on Egmont Key.

3

I turned wide back
to face the glittering iconic Skyway Bridge,
majestic guardian of Tampa Bay,
a lazy turn,
then throttled back
floating over the sparkling
silver-gold bridge updrafts,
became a glider,
recalled sailing beneath it sails full,
southwest wind. Like "Southern Cross" song,
evoking my brother, our favorite: "off the wind
on this heading, lie the Marquesas, we

got 80 feet of waterline, nicely making way"
What would he think of me now, a pilot?

4

More. The disease of more.
Was it this? Turning sharply back
toward St. Pete Whitted Airport,
the stall horn squawked, and soon
the deadly tug down,
as one wing stalled,
angling into downward corkscrew!
Panic set in, altitude only twelve hundred,
altitude is your friend, I winced, obey instructions
fear doesn't help
follow directions.
Still, fear gripped me.

In the Tomahawk manual,
I've studied it,
this danger requires counter-intuitive
action, acceleration down, down?

hard opposite rudder,
push on elevator yoke firm,
down, down, one turn, two
fear grips, but feel power restored, yes feel it

gain speed in descent, power levels both wings
oh, the welcome balance

at six hundred feet, pull up now! Level wings.
I will not forget.
A survival in perfect weather.
It might have been otherwise.
Not even a waterspout or
gust to explain, to blame.

5

Recovery, after a storm which wasn't a storm
following directions,
imagine that,
little rebel.

My brother would snicker, I think. Song lyric life continues:
"In a noisy bar in Avalon, I tried to call you...
but on a midnight watch I realized
why twice you ran away."
He understood it.

6

Level off easy.
Climb to eleven hundred feet.
I see sailboats
below.

I call into Whitted, "Two-four-one-eight-kilo
inbound at 1100 feet, 4 miles southeast,
information delta," hearing my own
fake "in charge" voice.

"Report two-mile base
runway 07, altimeter 30.02
wind one zero zero at thirteen.
Be advised sailboat mast on
approach 80 feet before displacement,"
his beacon voice replies; he
has been there forever, like
a lighthouse. Like my brother.

7

Recovery, a glow permeates my heart,
the sun's warmth a kind hand
on my shoulder,
I am safe, grateful,
guided by new experience, practice.

"One eight kilo, white Tomahawk,
two- mile base inbound zero seven,
information Delta," I say, steady.

"One eight kilo, clear to land.
call ground for FBO," tower brother says.

Sure, a little crosswind,
but gentle, gentle, flaps extend.
clear that huge mast,
who lets them park there?
gentle drop down, pull back
throttle, point to touchdown,

ease yoke back, float into the cradle,

welcome, 13 knots crosswind still
lifting from the Bay, crab in, kick slight left rudder, straighten, touch
tap brakes, no shimmy

the little plane eases
slowly to the turnoff,

the taxi is
like an awkward duck on land
after its flight, miracle
cushion landing, but
no splash.

8

Aging is sometimes
a childlike longing
as the shiny doors
down time's sepia corridors
gradually
click shut
behind me.

I'd almost closed my soul's door
on deep, abiding gratitude

for the chance to be here
one more day,

seeking the ground effect,
the soft cradle, home.

The Arrival of Childhood's End: Sci fi becomes fact, place

Advent, in place watching the signs:
one grandson wearing virtual reality goggles

waving a wand, commanding others
to drop their weapons,

while we decorate the tree, finish cookies
alone. NO—0 he shrieks at an enemy

we can't see. All the light surrounding him
is ours only. His lights are spectacular inside his brain

and I have no idea what outcomes
may be, a sci fi story
unfolding before my eyes,

what none of us can see.

My daughter says her son is helping others
online, gets thanks and praise from followers.

Yes, it is Advent, the time of expecting, waiting
for the child to save us, the light we can't yet see?

Try to embrace it. Along with my poem, I gave my granddaughter
three AI assisted poems with her college graduation gift.

We don't live in fear. I learned to fly an airplane
at sixty, a real one; it seemed a giant thing to soar

above the Gulf of Mexico, across aqua water, swirled by white sands,
landing in a real city taking that girl to lunch one birthday.

Boys now, post lockdown, don't really want anything more
than better gaming stuff, so we won't see the great Arrival.

September Flip Book Scenes, Flash Before the End

Getting ready to burn it down, start anew, save something, memory's
September teenage arc begins, whatever summer's dreams had
crushed, drowned, washed up in sand

consigned now to ashen, dusty corners. New
first clothes purchased with my saved allowance:
a matching, red-pleated wool skirt, cardigan

but school's first day dawned hot, sticky
humid yellow-brick junior high, my cherished choice all wrong
a sinful silly adolescent whim, my sumac allergies erupted skin.

At my locker, a thin boy shoved into my palm a many-folded note, graph
    paper,
tiny schematics for a rocket ship, a mini heart etched beneath; I ignored him,
    maker
 of spinning social studies mobiles, I still see circling: "Gentleman Johnny
Burgoyne Saratoga."

Years on, smoky leaves, I'm the new kid on campus, not yet 18
but great false ID, red wine made of me a princess, Sunday afternoon laughter,
furtive two, we drain DEKE frat house liquor cabinet Sunday afternoon,
blurry Cornell rooftop view.

September pregnant, grad school baby weighs heavy, single maternity top
    worn threadbare,
study seems irrelevant, that mile-long walk from Albany's parking lot a
    marathon,
I hum to the new man, "think I'm gonna have a son", ponder waxed paper
pressed maple leaf, "and that little boy is mine…"

First days of school, a mother and teacher now, again, again, again, decades spin
kids grow and thrive, some crises rise, a grandchild cries, a father dies, a boyfriend lies,
I learned to fly, but I still can't touch the sky, in dreams my brother's smile still high.

Decades flip furiously by. When school began with hurricane days in this strange tropic place,
replacing snow breaks with shooter lockdown drills, shrill bureaucratic ills, that
wildfire smoke and book burning, masked holidays, I began to wish for home.

Always September, I ponder openings, better than April, second chances, paradoxes like
dying to live, surrendering to win, giving to receive. I seek forgiveness.

Why couldn't I have been kinder to rocket boy? Where is he now?

Point au Roche, Lake Champlain

Steadfast Cedars at Point au Roche Middle Point

Endure, faith based

crawl forth

from granite face

to sea, beyond waves' frigid froth

Hope's race.

Curling cedar roots reach

round point, limbs clicking brittle,

icy bone gnarled, they teach

entwinement, long-term commitment

beach rock pointed south,

knows Place.

Trashcan Turkey

Winter ghost Dickens us now,
as ever, and my dead brother's birthday
looms to haunt. My first friend still
lends a hand at Thanksgiving:
Turkey in a Trashcan, a recipe
we birthed in the North woods long ago.

Turkey impaled on wood and metal stake,
the cross suggests a barbarity, a crucifixion,
a primitive rite, a vegetarian's nightmare
but once the trashcan's placed over it,
the Dutch oven formed, heaps of charcoal lit,
fire flames high, that twenty-pounder
done in two hours, smoky, juicy, succulent.
"Always use a metal trashcan, please," he'd say,
feign seriousness, peer over his wire-rimmed glasses.

That it removes so many bodies
from the kitchen for action outside,
allows for the peace of peeling potatoes, mashing
with buttermilk, butter, and
"Chives," I add at ghost's request,
"C'est magnifique!" whispers ghost.

I still have the pot he used to blend
his horseradish sauce, his finer gig trick,
unfiltered Camel smoke curling back
through nostrils, ring circling with breeze
round trip from cig clenched in teeth.
Measuring day's minutes in beer, nicotine,
suicide by twelve-pack, cartons.

He's still here, but the bones, the bones
to simmer winter stock with onion, Kosher salt,
minced carrots, celery, add fresh thyme, rosemary
after they're all gone, stir gently.

"Alas It Was to None but Me" *

Dad was miserable when I put him in the facility,
took no interest when
I tried to hang his WW2 Navy stuff, his Brown U basketball pics.
He couldn't get the catheter hooked up,
and the nurse said he'd have to learn to do it himself.
A former school principal, later professor, now 89,
he continually gazed across the pond
at the elementary school, wondering
if they needed him. Then he'd ask again for the car keys
I'd hidden.
My beloved alcoholic brother skulked around the parking lot,
refusing to enter, help or speak. I drove back home sobbing.
The next day's visit, Dad was calm at our lunch,
flirting with ladies. He checked his watch
the way he always had when he wanted me to go.

The next day's visit, he was in the hospital dying,
mouthing without words, needing to say, I knew not what
my brother again in the parking lot.
Outside, we hugged; our separate goodbyes done.
One month later, I spread two bags of ashes
over Tampa Bay, father, and son.
My brother's three sons, my son and daughter
played THE PARTING GLASS, and the Navy Hymn.
I danced an Irish jig on the boat deck.
All the long, humid night, I listened to the others
resting my head, the pillow a cairn.

* Title is lyrics from "The Parting Glass", famous Irish tune. ("Of all the harm that ere I did, alas it was to none but me.")

Passage Key, North of Anna Maria Island

Sunny Angel Wings

Empty pain knifed
through my abdomen,
behind my eyes'
blackness, a barely perceived candle burning brightly:
focus there, not the mustard painted concrete walls,
the beep-beep grind shift machine
scanning, right arm needled with putrid dye,
left arm raised back high, noises like grade B sci-fi,
I am the age
my mother was when she died,
I'm so surprised to be
almost dead, I was so healthy,
now just five days following
the second vax but no, the doc says,
not that, must be something else, more tests.
The mustard concrete, thick swirls, odd choice
for such a daunting experience, strange
silver hooks, cold so cold, but behold!

A painted angel, tattooed from dangling earrings
to bosom, shoulder to wrist, colorful wings
adorn her oh angel
delivers warm-warm blanket,
brings sunshine
bestows hope while
the machine clicks on, bless you
my angel, give my love to all the children,
my brother will welcome me, but
just before the light, that vision,
the wings on her back,
the sudden realization
the moment is now, warm,
the next not here yet.

Lake Champlain, Valcour Island

Reflections on Brochure of Home: Lake Champlain's "Adirondack Coast"

First open it: top picture, no, not like that, those blue-sky children holding baskets of strawberries,

no, it's dark mostly dark, not evil just poetic brooding, low hung clouds,

my wedding ring tossed among glacier remnants, ripples over black slate smooth, or

granite/limestone rocks with small holes worn by water's geologic drip time,

split seconds in human habitation, smiling children in Rulf's Pumpkin Patch, slate sky.

Yes, like that and apples, of course, always apples and beloved family pickers

returning each year, released like Persephone smiling spring.

Pine needle beds and woodsmoke, Adirondack peaks sing

happy hours driving home one-eyed those 1812 roads,

the miracle night arrivals up steep hill driveway.

Open summer vistas, tiny sails and rainbow spinnakers, Abenaki and Bluegrass.

Green and White Mountain Ranges on a clear day's route 9 pass.

Mohican wisdom with soundtrack scores, "No matter where

you go, I'll find you, if it takes a thousand years."

Those wide slatted leaning back outdoor chairs now called coastal,

we'd walk instead those autumn trails holding hands:
the nows of magic pass unnoticed,

crunchy, perfect maple leaf fire.

It's chilly so red hot chile simmers
when sumac gets fuzzy.

It spreads below old cemetery's hilltop,

those tiny graves of small ones, dead with mothers, simultaneous,

while newer, larger second-wife stones

mark the better fed,

tended tender

through the crystal winters,

not like the others

whose raw brittle fingers

still reach through now bare trees, click click

click their disease, still bitter-chilled after centuries.

Brochure is good card stock, though.

Heart loves New York in two languages.

Sturdy tan trifold with detail maps

noting seasonal icy road closures.

I bought that ring myself anyway,

its splash ripples this lake still.

Home is lake-polished black
igneous volcanic stones
shaped like smooth flat hearts
good for skipping.

And the Greatest of These Is Love

I loved watching my grandson's little fingers
slide up for the sharps, stretch down for the flats
unconcerned that the same keys could be
called either one, depending on key.
I said, "Try just playing a song with

all the black keys only,
        not falling down
to the white keys,"

tunes emerged,

harmonious and strange,

celebratory.

The finer points of
theory mattered little, stretching
left pinkie for E flat, the thumb for B Flat,
right pinkie E flat, thumb on G flat
He generated cool rhythms,

      syncopations, moving around black keys only

alternating hands, combinations.

While I knew some music teacher
would lecture the fun out of it all,
eventually, and TikTok would win
out with silly faces, stretched bodies,
horror and absurdity, knew that video games

would steal his mind when I
couldn't be there, I felt for a moment

it was a bit like prayer, meditation.
A call, then listening for response.

Someday, he might just sit down again, stay long enough
as I did finally, and it would save him, too.

Pantomime on the Doomed Mango Tree

Holding my breath, the decision pending,
I peek through aged windows
the man in the wheelchair,
waving wildly about the
task's enormity,
of removing the lovely tree
under which he
enjoys shade in 98 degrees,
pantomimes root structure,
canal seawall threat,
cost of project,
and how soon it must be done.

One crippled arm wiggle,
an atrophied root, the other
reaches round clawlike as though grabbing
from beneath.
A young man stands
on the seawall, sweaty shoulders
drooping, silent, grudging.
He does the old man's work,
but his body language conjures my brother,
asked to mow the lawn decades past.

For years, I have watched
and waited each summer
for these mangos,
unspeakably delicious, rare
fruit, like nothing in any store,
neighbors begging for a few,
eyeing the grapefruit-sized
rosy warm messages
from heaven.

I creep into
the cluttered garage,
eavesdrop as they move along,

hear the audio, finally,
and the sentence
pronounced upon
another old man,
a world traveler,
a hopeful diplomat,
who planted this tree
seventy years ago:
It's got to go. Decision.

Make way for the
millionaire tourists with
McMansions to rent out.

"Get a second opinion,"

I whisper to the universe.

Maybe the
man's handicap
taints his view. Pain
changes perception.
Maybe he's a mango hater.

Oh, loss and grief
are easier in pantomime,
preferably from distance.

We had to move.
A neighbor Facebooked
a picture of the empty lot.

Rattlesnake Mountain/Lake Champlain

Clarity

My dear friend

gives me three placemats

as a gift, from her Oaxaca travels

as she explains

quietly, our men

gabbing

in another room:

the blood tests

her bone marrow cancer,

remembers her own mother,

laments the result, suffering endless 'cures',

says she's had a fabulous life,

asks me to forgive

her decision

not to treat.

Taking my Morning Vitamins

Emptying a full glass of water
with the morning multi-v
a ritual worship of hope,
crossing my fingers
against the shadow of death,
time purchased, maybe?
Like buying a book that
supposes you've also bought
time to read it,
or subscribing
to a podcast buys time
to listen.
I love this ritual, anyway,
feel virtuous,
follow doctor's directions,
though that is pretty much the limit
of my obedience.
I seem plumb bent
otherwise
on my own destruction,
hiking mountains alone,
flying a small plane,
driving hundreds of miles
on Florida freeways
or an ADK mountain road
lonely dark single lanes
in a post-jam music glow,
night downpour again,
only one headlight
seems to show the
dim road ahead,
frightened deer
spring back sudden
shock frozen.

Ground Effect 2: Conversation With the One Who Knew Me Best, Once He's Gone, Please Forgive Me the Shock

I didn't have wings, could not fly to help.
I didn't have money, to bring you close.
I didn't have courage, to abandon all.
I didn't have vision, to see a clear solution.
I didn't have honor, to clear all obstacles, no matter what.
I didn't have counsel, to advise me how to choose.
I didn't have a father, so recently dead.
I didn't have a mother, so long ago gone.
I didn't have a husband, to direct and protect.
I didn't have self-esteem, so crushed by rejection.
I didn't have a God, so crucial to survival.

I lived in fear, I struggled with self-doubt,
I lived in anxiety; about things I couldn't change.
I lived without faith that all would be well
    in the end, and if things were not well
it was not yet the end.

The nurse said, "When he passed, I opened
the high window so his spirit could be free."

She is the one I most want to be:
who offers solace gently
when the guilt
just chokes me, I would be one who
coaxes fragile energy
sifts useless stress
offers still small voice
of home after flight.

Aerial Flight Tampa Bay

How to Survive a Hurricane from Far, Far Away

1. Remind her again to fill the tub with water.
2. Explain where the extra batteries are stored.
3. Provide the updated gate code.
4. Give telephone numbers of neighbors, the medics, the engineers.
5. Drain your bank account. Again.
6. Reassure her that she and your grandson are NOT homeless.
7. Enjoy an autumn hike, play some blue grassy music.
8. Try to decipher texts she sends frantically.
9. Explain the Keurig adaptation for loose coffee.
10. Watch horrific YouTube of destruction, places you've loved, people who matter.
11. Say, "When you lose power", not "If"
12. Remind her to check in with neighbors, even if all she wants to do is sleep.
13. If panic creeps into your voice, muffle, slur, obfuscate, coo something soothing.
14. Agree to watch a stupid violent series set in London with your partner.
15. Answer the emergency call at midnight, after power has been restored and the ambulance carrying her panic-attack friend has departed.
16. Ignore the nonsensical texts from the airline.
17. Trash that survivor's guilt.
18. Trash all guilt.
19. Thank your neighbors. In both places.
20. Be grateful that you never confided your true fear: the palm tree crashing through the front picture windows, crushing your sheltered family.
21. Her apartment washout is just a blessing in disguise.
22. Think of rainbows, unicorns, windfalls from   somewhere undamaged.

Reference Points: After the Hurricane

The lighthouse stands,
but the keeper's home, gone.
On the next corner, where we would turn to go for ice cream,
there is no corner.
There might not be ice cream for years, here.
On top of the seawall moved a mile in
from where it once protected someone's house,
rests a 50-foot cabin cruiser,
all its anchors and lines tossed about like
mysterious celestial spaghetti,
the flying monster's joke.

Not many roofs withstood
nine hours of 140 mph winds,
pounding, screeching, clawing first one direction
then the other.
"Historic" holds a different meaning,
connections to history so confused, distorted by news.
Some moment between once upon a time
and they lived.
They lived.
The miracle reference point.

A grand entry chandelier
offers welcome to sand,
Its fixtures dangling wires, while its sparkling glass remains intact.
Its home is gone, but it seems carefree in sunshine.
Not far away, a demolished bridge rebuilds in a week
Tribute to local faith and grit,
rejection of government contract and press doomsayers,
this lonely island gets Publix trucks the hungry seek.
Portable cell towers rise above the ruins for free, we hear.
Hope for many is the voice of a beloved friend, like a foghorn to sailors:
I am here. I am safe.
the only true reference points,
in the end.

Whiteface Overlook

We Uprooted Souls Seek

softly sinking air cushions,

sometimes wrenched from

social networks, our ancestors,

cherished mentors,

we float toward earth

seeking home,

grounded in physics,

but in magic too.

We are not ground down, grounds for,

grounds

Underground
don't forget this: our roots save us.

Wrap this. Fold carefully. Press to your heart.
Fertilize.
Find water, inhale air, light
Come home.
It opens
inside a bloom of hope,
a soft breeze
of protections,
the sturdy touch
of a kind hand
caressing the knotted shoulder
in early morning winter fog.

Faith, you are not alone, the next steps slow.

Open the door, smile, breathe in.

Exhale. Welcome home.

Acknowledgments

A variation of the poem, "Alas it Was to None But Me" and a version of "Pantomime of the Doomed Mango "appeared in *Turning Base: Wind Perceptions,* Mill City Press, 2018

Grateful appreciation for "Arrival of Childhood's End", a slightly different version, Middle West Press, "Giant Robot" anthology 2024, and "Reference Points after the Hurricane", Quill Keeper's Press, April 2024

A hearty and warm thanks to Rachel Baum, dear friend and poet, leader of "Moving Mountain Poets" of the Poets and Writers list, and members Julene, Karen, Linda, Eileen, Loretta, Dee, Carla, Lisa, Nina, and others.

A deep and abiding joy in remembering the support of my teacher friends, my "room" mates, partners in the long trudge. Jan, Tamia, you are always just around my peripheral vision, the warm hand, the sun on my shoulder, the secret garden, the rocking chair. And Kate, who climbed all the mountains, literally and figuratively, preparing a memoir in verse soon, my dear writer friend and longtime soul sister, Claudia Hornby, and all the Hornby's, for that matter. Maro Lorimer, my artistic muse, thank you for all these years. Recently departed spirit guide, Dr. Maria Pertik, you always come back. Whitcomb Garage jammers, JOY! Grateful appreciation to Leah Maines, Finishing Line Press, for guidance, suggestions, encouragement, acceptance. Bless you all.

Posthumous thanks to my family of origin, without whom I'd never have a story to tell. Elise Jouard Mullen, mom, a literature lover, pianist, singer, teacher. William B. Mullen, dad, a professor, high school principal, teacher, WW2 Navy hero, and best friend from birth, brother William Farel Mullen, a hospitality pro, writer, dreamer, haunted guy. And Glen Hoover, Vietnam Silver Star man, Farel's lifelong friend who supported him through thick and thin.

Thanks to my own children and grandchildren, firstborn son Finn, daughter Heidi, daughter in-law Meitra, first grandkid Maddy, second, Stella Richie, third, Max, and in-laws/outlaws Jackie and Casey. Thanks to nephews Cris, Andrew, Ryan, Nicholas, and Patty and Ken. You've all contributed much to making a sometimes-eccentric lady like me feel happy in my own skin.

And finally, most of all, my deepest gratitude to my best friend teacher, pilot, HP, and partner, Ed Sterba, for patience, tolerance, acceptance, and the ability to fix just about anything with a calm, soothing, cheerful voice, a wise solution, $700, a rifle, a pick-up truck, a list of tools, Czech-tech, love, and skill.

Betsy Lynch holds a BA in literature (Binghamton University) and M.S. (SUNY Albany) with extensive additional graduate credit in literature and linguistics from SUNY Plattsburgh, McGill, Indiana University, and the former St. Michael's College. Additional education in workshops such as Bread Loaf, Palm Beach Poetry, San Miguel de Allende Writers Festival, AWP, Florida Writers Association, recent "Kick Ass ADK Writers Festival" sponsored by the Adirondack Writing Center in Saranac Lake, numerous online and face-to-face conferences, readings, performances have fueled the creative fire.

After retiring from teaching English and ESL in New York State, she continued to teach English and ESL in overseas assignments and in Florida, retiring from the College of Central Florida in 2021. She has taught in Shanghai, China, Cusco, Peru, Quetzaltenango, Guatemala, and dual enrollment at several high schools.

While living on Anna Maria Island, her partner encouraged her to get her pilot's license, and she has been flying several small planes since 2012. She has found great joy in discovering the abundance of space, a new dimension, along with the challenges, uphill learning curves, and fear. Moving inland to an airpark community in central Florida was a choice that brought further challenge and great opportunity.

Born and raised in New Jersey, Long Island, and upstate New York, she considers the Adirondacks home, where she raised her children and taught. She divides her time between the Lake Champlain Region and Florida, where she and her best friend, Ed, fly a Piper Tomahawk named "Shadowfax" whenever they can.

Her children and grandchildren all live about an hour away.

A member of the "Moving Mountains Poets" (Poets and Writers Group led by Rachel Raum) for the last few years, she's been encouraged to assemble this collection. She has published a longer collection, *Turning Base: Wind Perceptions* (Mill City Press, 2018), and in numerous journals including including *Eclectica, Midwest Press, Quillkeepers Press, the Aerial Perspective, Sierra,* and *National Council of Teachers of English* (English Journal)

She may be reached
@BetsyTurnsBase (BetsyLynchWritespirit) on X
or through Finishing Line Press
or writespiritbetsylynch@gmail.com

www.ingramcontent.com/pod-product-compliance
Lightning Source LLC
Chambersburg PA
CBHW042311150426
43198CB00006B/118